C000062488

Supplicatory Canon and Akathist

To

Saint Xenia Fool for Christ
of St. Petersburg

Nun Christina
Anna Skoubourdis

Published by: Virgin Mary of Australia and Oceania 2023 ©
oceanitissa@gmail.com
www.oceanitissa.com.au
YouTube: Nun Christina Oceanitissa

All rights reserved. The material in this book may not be reproduced or distributed, in whole or in part, without the prior written permission of Virgin Mary of Australia and Oceania ©.

Dedicated to our dear friend

Ksenjia

Celebrates the 24th of January/6th of February

Troparion (Tone 4)

Having renounced the vanity of the earthly world,
Thou didst take up the cross of a homeless life of wandering;
Thou didst not fear grief, privation, nor the mockery of men,
And didst know the love of Christ.
Now taking sweet delight of this love in heaven,
O Xenia, the blessed and divinely wise,
Pray for the salvation of our souls.

Troparion (Tone 8)

In you, O mother was carefully preserved what is according to the image.
For you took up the Cross and followed Christ.
By so doing, you taught us to disregard the flesh for it passes away,
But to care instead for the soul since it is immortal.
Therefore, O Blessed Xenia, your spirit rejoices with the Angels.

Kontakion (Tone 3)

Having been as a wandering stranger on earth,
sighing for the heavenly homeland,
thou wast known as a fool by the senseless and unbelieving,
but as most wise and holy by the faithful,
and wast crowned by God with glory and honor,
O Xenia, courageous and divinely wise.
Therefore, we cry to thee:
Rejoice, for after earthly wandering thou hast come to dwell in the
Father's house.

Kontakion (Tone 7)

Having loved the poverty of Christ,
You are now being satisfied at the Immortal Banquet.
By the humility of the Cross, you received the power of God.
Having acquired the gift of miraculous help, O Blessed Xenia,
Beseech Christ God, that by repentance
We may be delivered from every evil thing.

Supplicatory Canon

Blessed is our God always, now and forever and to the ages of ages. Amen.

Psalm 142

O Lord, hear my prayer, give ear to my supplications in Your truth; hear me in Your righteousness. Do not enter into judgment, with Your servant, for in Your sight no one living is justified. For the enemy has persecuted my soul; he has crushed my life to the ground; he has made me dwell in darkness, like those who have long been dead, and my spirit is overwhelmed within me; my heart within me is distressed. I remembered the days of old; I meditated on all Your works: I pondered on the work of Your hands. I spread out my hands to You; my soul longs for You, like a thirsty land.

Hear me quickly, O Lord; my spirit fails. Do not turn Your face away from me, lest I be like those who go down into the pit. Cause me to hear Your mercy in the morning, for in You I have put my trust. Cause me to know, O Lord, the way in which I should walk, for I lift up my soul to You. Rescue me, lord, from my enemies; to You have I fled for refuge. Teach me to do Your will, for You are my God. Your good Spirit shall lead me in the land of uprightness. For Your name's sake, O Lord, You shall quicken me. In Your righteousness You shall bring my soul out of trouble, and in Your mercy, You shall utterly destroy my enemies. And you shall destroy all those who afflict my soul; for I am Your servant.

Tone 4

God is the Lord and has revealed Himself to us; blessed is He who comes in the name of the Lord.

Give thanks to the Lord for He is good, for His mercy endures forever.

God is the Lord and has revealed Himself to us; blessed is He who comes in the name of the Lord.

All the nations have surrounded me, but in the name of the Lord, I have overcome them.

God is the Lord and has revealed Himself to us; blessed is He who comes in the name of the Lord.

This has been done by the Lord, and it is wonderful in our eyes.

God is the Lord and has revealed Himself to us; blessed is He who comes in the name of the Lord.

Troparia.
Mode 4. You who were lifted.

As a partaker of the joy of the Lord, and a participant in the divine tabernacle, always pray, we beseech you, that we may be delivered from trials, dangers, and terrible afflictions, O most blessed Xenia, we who approach you with faith, fervently intercede for us, O most venerable.

Glory to the Father and the Son and the Holy Spirit.

Repeat the above or the Apolytikion of the Church

Now and forever and to the ages of ages. Amen.

Theotokion
O Theotokos, we shall never be silent .of your mighty acts, all we the unworthy; *had you not stood to intercede for us .who would have delivered us, from the numerous perils? .Who would have preserved us all .until now with our freedom? .O Lady, we shall not depart from you; .for you always save your servants, from all tribulation.

Psalm 50

Have mercy on me, O God, according to Your great mercy; and according to the multitude of Your compassion blot out my transgression. Wash me thoroughly from my iniquity and cleanse me from my sin. For I acknowledge my iniquity, and my sin is ever before me. Against You, You only, have I sinned, and done this evil in Your sight, that You may be found just when You speak, and blameless when You are judged. For behold, I was conceived in iniquities, and in sins my mother bore me.

For behold, You have loved truth: You have made known to me the secret things of Your wisdom. You shall sprinkle me with hyssop, and I shall be made clean: You shall wash me, and I shall be whiter than snow. Make me to hear joy and gladness, that bones which You have broken may rejoice. Turn Your face away from my sins and blot out all my iniquities. Create in me a clean heart, O God, and renew a steadfast spirit within me. Do not cast me away from Your presence, and do not take Your Holy Spirit from me. Restore to me the joy of Your salvation: And establish me with Your governing Spirit.

I shall teach transgressors Your ways, and the ungodly shall turn back to You. Deliver me from bloodguiltiness, O God, the God of my salvation, my tongue shall rejoice in Your righteousness. O Lord open my lips, and my mouth shall show forth Your praise. For if You had desired sacrifice, I would give it: You do not delight in burnt offering. A sacrifice to God is a broken spirit, God will not despise a broken and humbled heart.

Do good in Your good pleasure to Sion; and let the walls of Jerusalem be built. Then You shall be pleased with a sacrifice of righteousness, with oblation and whole burnt offerings. Then they shall offer bulls on Your altar.

Plagal of the Fourth Tone

Ode One
Crossing the waters.

Saint of God intercede for us.

O Xenia, God-bearer, you lived as a foreigner and stranger in this life, touching the hearts of the faithful, with your strange life, O holy one, protect me from diverse calamities and afflictions.

Saint of God intercede for us.

Xenia, full of Grace, have mercy on me, I who plead to you in distress, and send forth your mercy on all who plead for your divine intercessions.

Glory to the Father, the Son and the Holy Spirit.

O holy Mother, you who is filled with Divine Grace, pour upon me, the sweet nectar of Grace, so that I may shake off the poison of sin and the bitterness caused by the passions.

Now and forever and to the ages of ages.

Just as the Virgin gave birth to the Poet who redeemed the world from the condemnation of Adam, deliver my wretched soul from the bondage and affliction of the passions.

Ode Three
The apse of the heavens.

Saint of God intercede for

Having died to the world in Christ, you lived, O Holy Xenia, a holy life, therefore, put to death the dreadful sin that lives within my heart, and fortify my mind with the fear of God.

Saint of God intercede for us.

O Mother, when we are in danger and suffering greatly, hasten to deliver us quickly from the tempests of trials and circumstances, O all-praised Xenia, and protect us from all afflictions that may harm us, we implore you.

Glory to the Father, the Son and the Holy Spirit.

O blessed Xenia, please intercede, that Jesus the Saviour and Lord of all may grant forgiveness of our sins, reconciliation, and peace to all we who run to you in faith, pleading for your protection.

Now and forever and to the ages of ages.

O Theotokos, deliver me from the power of the evil one, through whom my soul is defiled by words and deeds, and guide me towards repentance, so that I may be made worthy to enter into Eternal Life.

Deliver, O Holy Xenia, through your prayers to our Creator, from all affliction and tribulation, we you plead to you, for your divine protection.

Look graciously upon your servant, all-praiseworthy Theotokos, and upon my painful physical suffering, and remedy my anguish of spirit.

PRIEST

Have mercy on us, O God, according to Your great mercy, we pray You, hear us and have mercy.
(Lord, have mercy. (x3)
Let us pray for pious and Orthodox Christians.
(Lord, have mercy. (x3)
Again we pray for (episcopal rank) (name).
(Lord, have mercy. (x3)
Again we pray for mercy, life, peace, health, salvation, protection, forgiveness, and remission of the sins of the servants of God, all pious Orthodox Christians residing and visiting in this city: the parishioners, the members of the parish council, the stewards, and benefactors of this holy church.
(Lord, have mercy. (x3)
Again we pray for the servants of God... (At this time the Priest commemorates those for whom the Paraklesis is sung.)
(Lord, have mercy. (x3)
Again we pray for those who bear fruit and do good works in this holy and all venerable church, for those who labor and those who sing, and for the people here present who await Your great and rich mercy.
(Lord, have mercy. (x3)
For You are a merciful God Who loves mankind, and to You we offer up glory, to the Father and to the Son and to the Holy Spirit, now and forever and to the ages of ages.
(Amen.)

Kathisma in the Second Tone
A fervent prayer...

Having led a foreign life in a manner befitting a stranger, you were deemed worthy of many gifts from Christ, through which, O divine Xenia, deliver from trials and dangers those who seek your help, and soothe the struggles of your children who praise you, O holy Mother.

Ode Four
O Lord, I have heard of.

Saint of God intercede for us.

Intercede before the All-compassionate Christ, O God-bearing Xenia, for the healing of our souls, which have been wounded by sin.

Saint of God intercede for us.

We implore you, O Xenia, to ask for the healing of diseases, the deliverance from all kinds of afflictions, and the forgiveness of sins on our behalf.

Glory to the Father, the Son and the Holy Spirit

As you overcame the foolishness of the evil one, with your Grace inspired life, O Mother, shatter also the foolishness of the adversary that is within me.

Now and forever and to the ages of ages.

Having been deadened by the passions, revive me, O Virgin, I implore You, who bore the truly Eternal life, Christ, in your flesh.

Ode Five
Lord, enlighten us.

Saint of God intercede for us.

Alienate us from the thoughts of the adversary and make us familiar with the fear of God, O holy Xenia, and fill our hearts with the Glory of God.

Saint of God intercede for us.

Having great boldness before the Lord, whom you glorified in your noble life, do not be lacking in fulfilling every request of ours, O holy one.

Glory to the Father the Son and the Holy Spirit.

You lived by the law of God, a life with love and much patience, O Mother Xenia, strengthen those who run to you for protection.

Now and forever and to the ages of ages.

You have dawned upon us, the Eternal Light, from your womb, O Mother of God, the bearer of light, Mary. Therefore, scatter the darkness of my mind.

Ode Six

My petition.

Saint of God intercede for us.

Having completed the greatest struggles and attained perfect understanding, deliver me from adversary and tribulation, O Mother, we who magnify your life, and grant us great gifts and miracles, and divine inspiration, through your intercessions.

Saint of God intercede for us.

O Mother Xenia, you received from Christ, the great gift of miracles, therefore, your tomb always pours forth healings for both souls and bodies, I implore you to heal me who am sick in both, O God-inspired one.

Glory to the Father, the Son and the Holy Spirit.

Holy one, grant me strength, with your intercession to be rescued from all corruption, impure thoughts and passions, so that in old age I may live a virtuous life and obtain Eternal Life through Christ's goodness.

Now and forever and to the ages of ages.

O Virgin, Mother of God, the highest throne, the ever-virgin Daughter, the sure salvation of sinners, raise me up from the lowest pit of sins and passions to true repentance.

Deliver, O Holy Xenia, through your prayer to our Creator, from all affliction and tribulation, we who plead to you, for your divine protection.

Entreat for us, O spotless Maiden who gave birth to the divine Word, inexplicably through a word in the latter days, since you indeed, speak with motherly freedom.

PRIEST
Have mercy on us, O God, according to Your great mercy, we pray You, hear us and have mercy.
(Lord, have mercy. (x3)
Let us pray for pious and Orthodox Christians.
(Lord, have mercy. (x3)

Again we pray for (episcopal rank) (name).
(Lord, have mercy. (x3)
Again we pray for mercy, life, peace, health, salvation, protection, forgiveness, and remission of the sins of the servants of God, all pious Orthodox Christians residing and visiting in this city: the parishioners, the members of the parish council, the stewards, and benefactors of this holy church.
(Lord, have mercy. (x3)
Again we pray for the servants of God... (At this time the Priest commemorates those for whom the Paraklesis is sung.)
(Lord, have mercy. (x3)
Again we pray for those who bear fruit and do good works in this holy and all venerable church, for those who labor and those who sing, and for the people here present who await Your great and rich mercy.
(Lord, have mercy. (x3)
For You are a merciful God Who loves mankind, and to You we offer up glory, to the Father and to the Son and to the Holy Spirit, now and forever and to the ages of ages.
(Amen.)

Kontakion
Tone 2. Of your blood.
Your foreign way of life, has been glorified, O holy one, you saw the hidden mysteries of Christ, and have been endowed by the Life-giver, abundant spiritual gifts, thus grant the requests of those who honour you.

Prokeimenon.
I waited patiently for the Lord, and He heeded me. He heard my supplication. (2)

Verse: He set my foot on a rock and directed my steps.

PRIEST
Let us pray to the Lord our God that we may be made worthy to hear the holy Gospel.
(Lord, have mercy. (x3)

Wisdom. Arise. Let us hear the Holy Gospel.
Peace be with all.
(And with your spirit.)

The reading is from the Gospel according to Matthew. (11:27-30)

Let us be attentive.
(Glory to You, O Lord. Glory to You.)

All things have been delivered to Me by My Father, and no one knows the Son except the Father. Nor does anyone know the Father except the Son, and the one to whom the Son wills to reveal Him. Come to Me, all you who labor and are heavy laden, and I will give you rest. Take My yoke upon you and learn from Me, for I am gentle and lowly in heart, and you will find rest for your souls. For My yoke is easy and My burden is light."
(Glory to You, O Lord. Glory to You.)

Second Tone

Glory to the Father and the Son and the Holy Spirit.

Through the prayers of the Saint, O Merciful One, blot out the multitude of mine offences.

Both now and forever and to the ages of ages. Amen.

Through the intercessions of the Theotokos, merciful One, wash away my many personal offenses.

Verse: Have mercy on me, O God, according to Your great mercy; and according to the abundance of Your compassion, blot out my transgression.

Plagal of the Second Tone
Having laid all their hope.

O holy Xenia, fragrant flower of Russia, treasure of virtues, and precious vessel of Divine Grace, please intercede fervently to Christ to save us from all evil, danger, distress, and affliction, we seek your help and grace, asking for the gift of Divine compassion and the remission of our sins, as well as for Divine mercy.

Ode Seven
Coming out of Judea.

Saint of God intercede for us.

Those who come to your tomb, Mother, receive grace through faith, therefore, grant healing to us who cry out for the healing of our souls and bodies, blessed is our God, the God of our Fathers.

Saint of God intercede for us.

O Xenia, crush the proud serpent that rises up against us, and grant every good deed and steadfast peace to those who cry out to you, blessed is our God, the God of our Fathers.

Glory to the Father, the Son and the Holy Spirit.

O God-bearing one, with divine fear cultivate the seeds of virtue, and grant strength from on high and power in all things to those who sing in unison, blessed is our God, the God of our Fathers.

Now and forever and to the ages of ages.

From the bitter habit of sinning, O Virgin, draw my mind to the light of repentance, guiding me to cry out to You in faith, Hail, all-radiant lamp of the unfading light.

Ode Eight
The King of heaven.

Saint of God intercede for us.

Grant healing, O Russian saint, to my ailing soul and heal the pain of my body through your God-given grace, O blessed one.

Saint of God intercede for us.

O Xenia, through your life of holy foolishness, you sanctified your thoughts, thus holy one, calm the evil thoughts that overshadow us.

Glory to the Father, the Son and the Holy Spirit.

O Holy One, protect those who seek your divine help in all kinds of trials, granting us the remission of our sins, through your divine intercessions.

Now and forever and to the ages of ages.

Grant me strength to trample the deceitful one, O Theotokos, and his destructive power, so that I may glorify you, the one who is full of grace.

Ode Nine
Saved through you.

Saint of God intercede for us.

O ever-blessed Xenia, sustain those who honour you and free them from the madness of the evil one and the snares of many scandals.

Saint of God intercede for us.

Your tomb pours forth healing for all, and now may your intercession be for us a source of heavenly joy, O God-inspired Xenia.

Glory to the Father, the Son and the Holy Spirit.

O Holy Xenia, from the streams of life-giving waters that flow from the springs, let a drop of salvation refresh my heart.

Now and forever and to the ages of ages.

We praise you, O Theotokos, for your glorious childbirth, through which we were delivered from corruption and death, for you, O Maiden, gave birth to the Ruler of life.

Megalynaria.

Truly you are worthy to be blessed, Mother of our God, the Theotokos, you the ever blessed one, and all blameless one, .and the Mother of our God. You are honoured more than the Cherubim, and you have more glory, when compared, to the Seraphim. You, without corruption, did bear God, the Logos. You are the Theotokos. You do we magnify.

Rejoice, O fellow of the Saints! Rejoice, foolishness that overcomes the cunning one, hospitality that drives away the evil one, and through Christ, receiving the gifts of Holy Spirit, help us to live steadfast.

Having cast away material things, Mother, you put on the spiritual struggle, which you completed perfectly, as a stranger in the midst of the world, you brilliantly practiced.

Rejoice now, O all-blessed Xenia, in the tabernacles of the heavens, from there, redeem us, and do not cease to deliver us from all sorrow and dejection.

You accomplished the great struggle in the world with patience, as one without flesh in the flesh, therefore, O Xenia, you were deemed worthy of heavenly rewards, please ask for the forgiveness of our sins.

Through a divine intervention, your tomb bears abundant healings for those who approach it with reverence, therefore, O Mother, labor to cure those who are weak in both soul and body from the wounds of sins.

O Mother, having the greatest confidence towards Christ, intercede earnestly for us, O blessed Xenia, to save us from danger and every grievous harm.

With the hosts of Angels, God's messengers, with the Lord's Forerunner, and Apostles, the chosen twelve, with the saints most holy, and with you, the Theotokos, we seek your intercession for our salvation.

Trisagion

Holy God, Holy Mighty, Holy Immortal, have mercy on us. (x3)

Glory to the Father and the Son and the Holy Spirit. Both now and ever and to the ages of ages. Amen.

All-holy Trinity, have mercy on us. Lord, forgive our sins. Master, pardon our transgressions. Holy One, visit and heal our infirmities for your name's sake.

Lord, have mercy. (x3)

Glory to the Father and the Son and the Holy Spirit. Both now and ever and to the ages of ages. Amen.

Our Father, who art in heaven, hallowed be Your name. Your kingdom come, Your will be done, on earth as it is in heaven. Give us this day our daily bread; and forgive us our trespasses, as we forgive those who trespass against us. And lead us not into temptation, but deliver us from evil. Amen.

Mode pl. 2.
Have mercy on us, Lord have mercy on us.

For with nothing to say in our own defence, we sinners offer this supplication to you our Master. Have mercy on us.

Glory to the Father, the Son and the Holy Spirit.

Lord have mercy on us, for in You we trust.

Be not enraged with us greatly, nor remember our iniquities. But look upon us now, being compassionate, and deliver us from our enemies. For You are our God, and we Your people, all of us the work of Your hands, and now we have invoked Your name.

Now and forever and to the ages of ages. Amen.

Theotokion.
Open the gate of compassion for us, O blessed Theotokos. For hoping in you, let us not fail in our aim. Through you may we be delivered from adversities. For you are the salvation of the Christian race.

Apolytikion. Plagal 1.

You lived in the world as a stranger, O Xenia, and steadfastly defeated the sophist of wickedness through your foolish pretenses with a godly mind, therefore you received from God the gift to see far-off things and to predict them clearly, having departed from this life, you joined the choirs of the Saints."

Second Tone
Joseph took you down.

O Xenia, having lived a life wounded by the love of Christ and having received the gift of miracles by God, you are greatly praised, you provide swift assistance to those in need of your protection with a powerful strength, therefore, we implore you, O Mother, to fulfil all our sincere requests, we who praise you.

Lady, do you receive, from your servants, their many prayers; .and deliver all of us, from all sadness and necessity.

My numerous hopes are placed, before you, most holy One; Mother of our God, guard me with care, within your sheltered arms.

PRIEST
Through the prayers of our holy fathers, Lord Jesus Christ, our God, have mercy on us and save us.
(Amen.)

Akathist

Kontakion 1
Blessed Mother Xenia, Holy Fool for the sake of Christ, you elected to undergo the struggle of patience and the suffering of affliction. We therefore honor your sacred memory with hymns of praise. Help us against our enemies, visible and invisible, that we may cry to you:

Rejoice, Blessed Xenia, faithful intercessor for our souls.

Ikos 1
After the death of your husband, blessed mother, you sought the life of the angels and rejected the beauty of this world and all that is in it — the desire of the eyes, the lust of the flesh, and the pride of life. Instead, you acquired the understanding of Christ our Savior. We therefore appeal to your loving-kindness, that you will hear these praises which we now offer you.

Rejoice, for you were a peer of Saint Andrew, the Holy Fool for Christ.
Rejoice, for you renounced your own name, referring to yourself as dead.
Rejoice, for you assumed foolishness and took the name of your departed husband, Andrei.
Rejoice, for you called yourself by a man's name, renouncing pride and vanity.
Rejoice, for you accepted voluntary poverty for the sake of Christ.
Rejoice, for you distributed all your substance to good people and to the poor.
Rejoice, for you comfort all those who turn to you in prayer.
Rejoice, for you quickly help in times of trouble and despair.
Rejoice, for your holy foolishness has taught us to reject the vain wisdom of this age.
Rejoice, for you were full of wisdom transcending this world.
Rejoice, for you preferred mockery and ridicule to earthly glory.
Rejoice, for you have been glorified by God.
Rejoice, Blessed Xenia, faithful intercessor for our souls.

Kontakion 2
Perceiving your way of life as strange, for you spurned the comforts of home and all worldly riches, O blessed mother, your kinsmen thought you were deranged. Yet, the people of St. Petersburg, seeing your humility, lack of acquisitiveness, and voluntary poverty, sang to God: Alleluia.

Ikos 2

Blessed Xenia, you hid the understanding given to you by God under an apparent mindlessness. Amid the vanity of a great city you lived like a desert-dweller, unceasingly offering your prayers to God. Marveling at your way of life, we cry out to you in praise:

Rejoice, for you took upon your shoulders the heavy cross of foolishness which God had given to you.
Rejoice, for you bore it without hesitation.
Rejoice, for you hid the radiance of grace under an assumed insanity.
Rejoice, for your foolishness was most wise.
Rejoice, for you acquired the gift of clairvoyance through extreme humility and feats of prayer.
Rejoice, for you showed forth this gift for the benefit and salvation of those who suffer and struggle.
Rejoice, for you beheld the sufferings of the people clairvoyantly, as from afar.
Rejoice, for your prayers brought relief to those in pain and distress.
Rejoice, for you prophesied to the good woman the birth of a son.
Rejoice, for you implored God that He grant the woman a child.
Rejoice, for you hurry to entreat the Lord in behalf of your neighbors.
Rejoice, for you have taught all the faithful to flee to God in prayer.
Rejoice, Blessed Xenia, faithful intercessor for our souls.

Kontakion 3

By the power given to you by God from on high, you manfully endured burning heat and bitter cold, crucifying the flesh with its passions and lusts. Mercifully enlightened by the Holy Spirit, you gratefully cried out unceasingly to God: Alleluia.

Ikos 3

With the sky as your roof and the earth as your bed, Blessed Xenia, you spurned the pleasures of the flesh for the sake of the Kingdom of God. Beholding the holiness of your manner of life, we humbly cry out to you with compunction:

Rejoice, for you gave your earthly home to the people.
Rejoice, for you sought and received the shelter of Heaven.
Rejoice, for you possessed nothing that was earthly, but enriched all spiritually.
Rejoice, for you became a treasure house of the gifts of Heaven.

Rejoice, for you counted every material thing as nothing.
Rejoice, for you were thereby freed from every loss.
Rejoice, for you endured hunger and cold in ragged clothing.
Rejoice, for you have been adorned with the fruits of piety.
Rejoice, by your afflictions you teach the people endurance.
Rejoice, by your struggles you show the world patience.
Rejoice, our compassionate deliverer from the turmoil of this world.
Rejoice, our fervent advocate before the Throne of the Most High.
Rejoice, Blessed Xenia, faithful intercessor for our souls.

Kontakion 4

The tempest of life which assailed St. Petersburg, you weathered by meekness and guilelessness, O blessed mother. You thereby acquired dispassion toward this corrupt world and thus sang to God: Alleluia.

Ikos 4

Hearing of your endurance of a multitude of afflictions for the sake of Christ, and that you comfort the sorrowful, strengthen the weak, and guide the lost to walk on the straight path — the suffering people hasten to seek your aid and to sing to you in this manner:

Rejoice, for you loved the path of Christ with all your heart.
Rejoice, for you gladly bore the Cross of Christ.
Rejoice, for you endured every offense hurled at you by the world, the flesh and the devil.
Rejoice, for you thus emulated the ascetics of the desert.
Rejoice, for you were filled to overflowing with the gifts of God.
Rejoice, for you freely bestow spiritual gifts upon those in need.
Rejoice, for you displayed love for your neighbors.
Rejoice, for you provided consolation for the suffering.
Rejoice, for you shed unceasing tears of repentance.
Rejoice, for you wipe away the tears of those who sorrow.
Rejoice, for you sought neither comfort nor warmth for yourself.
Rejoice, for you were wondrously warmed by the grace of the Holy Spirit.
Rejoice, Blessed Xenia, faithful intercessor for our souls.

Kontakion 5

Your life of holiness, Blessed Xenia, illumined the sky of St. Petersburg, like a divinely guided star. To all those perishing in the madness of sin you showed the path of salvation, calling them to repentance that they might cry acceptably to God: Alleluia.

Ikos 5

Seeing your feats of prayer and your endurance of heat and cold, pious folk sought to alleviate your hardship by offering you clothing and food. You then distributed all these things to the poor, Blessed Xenia, desiring to maintain your spiritual struggle. Full of wonder at your voluntary poverty, we cry out to you thus:

Rejoice, for you willingly endured burning heat and freezing cold for the sake of Christ.
Rejoice, for you were warmed by the indwelling of the Holy Spirit.
Rejoice, for you remained continually in prayer.
Rejoice, for you never tire of interceding for mankind.
Rejoice, for in all-night vigils you prayed for the city of St. Petersburg.
Rejoice, for many times you preserved it from the wrath of God.
Rejoice, for every day of the year you prayed at night in a field.
Rejoice, for you warmed the cold earth with your fervent tears.
Rejoice, for in poverty of spirit you tasted the sweetness of Paradise.
Rejoice, for in this sweetness you left behind all earthly things.
Rejoice, for you abide wholly in God.
Rejoice, for you delight in the bridal banquet of your Master.
Rejoice, Blessed Xenia, faithful intercessor for our souls.

Kontakion 6

All who have been delivered by you from different ailments, misfortunes and sorrows — the rich and the poor, the old and the young — proclaim the holiness of your life, O Holy Fool for Christ. In like manner, we glorify you and cry out to God in gratitude: Alleluia.

Ikos 6

The glory of your struggles shone forth, holy mother, when at night you secretly carried stones for those who were constructing the Church of the Smolensk Icon of the Mother of God, easing the tasks of the builders. Mindful of this, we sinners reverently cry out to you such things as these:

Rejoice, blessed and righteous model of feats of piety.
Rejoice, for you teach us to perform virtuous deeds in secret.
Rejoice, devoted caretaker of the holiness of the Church.
Rejoice, for you aided those who were building the Church of God.
Rejoice, zealous laborer for the Lord of the vineyard.
Rejoice, for you ease our labors on the path of salvation.
Rejoice, heavenly aid of the city of St. Petersburg.

Rejoice, for you sanctified your city by your painful footsteps.

Rejoice, tranquility of those who have recourse to you in prayer.

Rejoice, for you comfort all the sorrowful.

Rejoice, Holy Fool who continually calls on the Name of the Lord.

Rejoice, for you thereby rest in Christ your Master.

Rejoice, Blessed Xenia, faithful intercessor for our souls.

Kontakion 7

Desiring to deliver from sorrow the mourning physician who had buried his wife, you commanded a certain maiden to hasten to Okhta. She was to take him as her husband and console him. This they did as you said, singing to God in joy: Alleluia.

Ikos 7

A new wonder you revealed in your prayer, blessed mother, when you said to a pious woman, "Take a five-kopek piece, and it will go out," thus prophesying that a fire would strike her house. At your supplication, the flame of the fire was extinguished. Amazed by your holiness, we cry out praises to you:

Rejoice, for you unceasingly mourned over your sins.

Rejoice, for you bore suffering in body and soul.

Rejoice, for you extinguish the sorrows of the people.

Rejoice, for you show forth boldness before God for the suffering.

Rejoice, virtuous lamp burning brightly in prayer to God.

Rejoice, strong intercessor amid misfortunes and perils.

Rejoice, for you save from perdition those beset by the passions.

Rejoice, for you crucified your flesh with constant mortification.

Rejoice, for you turn pious virgins away from marriage with unbelievers.

Rejoice, for you deliver from despair those who have been wounded by a wicked curse.

Rejoice, righteous defender of those falsely accused.

Rejoice, for your defender is the Most High.

Rejoice, Blessed Xenia, faithful intercessor for our souls.

Kontakion 8

As a homeless wanderer you trod the path of your life in the capital city of Russia, bearing afflictions and reproaches with great patience. Now, abiding in the heavenly Jerusalem, with joy you sing to God: Alleluia.

Ikos 8

You were all things to all people, O Blessed Xenia — comfort for the sorrowful, protection and defense for the weak, joy for the grieving, clothing for the poor, and healing for the sick. Let us then cry to you:

Rejoice, through holy foolishness you ascended to the Kingdom.
Rejoice, through homelessness you acquired a mansion on high.
Rejoice, intercessor in Heaven for us mortals suffering on earth.
Rejoice, dependable provider of our every need.
Rejoice, holy mother who shows us a model of service to God.
Rejoice, Holy Fool who endured much affliction and grief in this world.
Rejoice, defender of the tormented ones who pray to you.
Rejoice, protectress of the persecuted and oppressed.
Rejoice, for you rebuke those who abuse their fellows.
Rejoice, for you put to shame unbelievers and those who babble.
Rejoice, for you were clothed in rags and tatters.
Rejoice, for God has adorned you with the splendid raiment of righteousness.
Rejoice, Blessed Xenia, faithful intercessor for our souls.

Kontakion 9
Blessed mother, you endured all illness, bodily poverty, hunger and thirst, and the reproach of iniquitous people who considered you to be insane. Yet, praying to the Lord, you continually cried out to Him: Alleluia.

Ikos 9
Even the most eloquent orators are unable to understand how by your holy foolishness you reproved the madness of this world, and how by your weakness you put the mighty of this world to shame. They do not know the power and wisdom of God which are in you. Even we, who thereby receive your aid, can only sing to you such things as these:

Rejoice, potent bearer of the Divine Spirit.
Rejoice, along with the Apostle Paul you boasted in your weakness.
Rejoice, for you reproved the world by your feigned foolishness.
Rejoice, for you spurned the glamour of this world for the sake of salvation and the Kingdom.
Rejoice, for you disdained the beautiful things of this earth.
Rejoice, for you loved the good things of Heaven with all your heart.
Rejoice, for you were attentive to the inner voice of the Lord.
Rejoice, for you call us to the narrow path of salvation.
Rejoice, dread denouncer of drunkenness as a sin.

Rejoice, holy protectress of the Orthodox family.
Rejoice, for you were renowned for your kindness and love.
Rejoice, for in Christ you found comfort for your sorrows.
Rejoice, Blessed Xenia, faithful intercessor for our souls.

Kontakion 10
Yearning to save your soul, you crucified the flesh with its passions and lusts. Utterly denying yourself, you carried your cross upon your shoulders and followed after Christ with all your heart, singing to Him: Alleluia.

Ikos 10
You are a firm rampart and an unassailable refuge for those who pray to you, Mother Xenia. We therefore implore you, by your supplications help us against our enemies visible and invisible, so that we may cry to you:

Rejoice, for you worked diligently in the garden of Christ.
Rejoice, for you move us to spiritual labor.
Rejoice, through steadfastness of faith you resisted the devil's snares.
Rejoice, through holy foolishness you discerned the wiles of the enemy.
Rejoice, for you bring the peace of God into the homes of Christians.
Rejoice, by heavenly confidence you impart blessings to good children.
Rejoice, for you extinguish the spirit of despair in the hearts of the oppressed.
Rejoice, by mystic supplication you relieve their burdens.
Rejoice, for you have shone forth the mercy of God upon the afflicted of the world.
Rejoice, by unceasing prayer you shed rays of Christian love upon all.
Rejoice, for you offered yourself to God like incense in a censer.
Rejoice, by the cross of asceticism you attained heavenly wisdom.
Rejoice, Blessed Xenia, faithful intercessor for our souls.

Kontakion 11
Those who have been saved from misfortune, affliction, sorrow, and every kind of danger offer you hymns of praise, holy mother, and together with the saints and angels we sing to God: Alleluia.

Ikos 11
Your holy foolishness, O Blessed Xenia, has been shown to be a radiant light illumining the people amid the darkness of this world. You have

delivered those who have fallen into the mire of sin, and directed their path to the light of Christ. We therefore lovingly cry out to you:

Rejoice, by your manner of life you amazed the angels.
Rejoice, for while in the world, you lived above the world.
Rejoice, by your many labors you acquired great grace.
Rejoice, for your ways were those of an ascetic of the wilderness.
Rejoice, for you enlighten Christians with the light of God.
Rejoice, for you shone forth with the grace of God over the darkness of sin.
Rejoice, for you put to shame the spirits of malice.
Rejoice, for you set your hope on the Almighty.
Rejoice, for you were clad in the brilliant robe of unwavering faith.
Rejoice, for on the straight path of salvation you give a helping hand to the desperate.
Rejoice, for you strengthen those who are weak in faith.
Rejoice, for you were renowned for your kindness and love.
Rejoice, for you put to shame the spirits of malice.
Rejoice, Blessed Xenia, faithful intercessor for our souls.

Kontakion 12
You pour forth grace in abundance upon those who honor your memory and flee to your protection, O Blessed Xenia. Likewise, upon us who pray to you now, do also pour forth streams of healing from God, so that we may acceptably cry out to Him: Alleluia.

Ikos 12
Hymning your many wonders, blessed mother, we praise you and entreat you with all our heart. Forsake not us sinners amid our grievous circumstances, but beseech the Lord of hosts that we fall not away from the True Faith. Rather, strengthened in it by your prayers, we gratefully cry out to you:

Rejoice, for you instruct us to crucify the flesh, together with the passions and lusts.
Rejoice, for you come to our aid amid every spiritual battle.
Rejoice, for you teach us to have sympathy for the suffering.
Rejoice, for you bear our infirmities with all your heart.
Rejoice, for you hear our supplications day and night.
Rejoice, for you ever mediate the salvation of your people.
Rejoice, for you protect those who honor your memory.
Rejoice, for you give joy to those who hasten to your tomb.

Rejoice, for you traveled the path of tribulation.
Rejoice, for you thereby obtained everlasting salvation.
Rejoice, for your light has shone forth before all.
Rejoice, for you dispel the darkness of sin, together with confusion and doubt.
Rejoice, Blessed Xenia, faithful intercessor for our souls.

Kontakion 13
Holy and blessed Mother Xenia, as you bore a heavy cross during your lifetime, accept from us sinners this entreaty which we offer you. By your supplications, protect us from the assaults of the spirits of darkness and from all who plot evils against us. Beseech our most compassionate God to grant us power and might, so that we may bear our own crosses. Let us follow Christ our Lord, and go forth singing with you to Him:

Alleluia. Alleluia. Alleluia.

(Repeat the above Kontakion 13, 3x)
(Then continue below)

Ikos 1
After the death of your husband, blessed mother, you sought the life of the angels and rejected the beauty of this world and all that is in it — the desire of the eyes, the lust of the flesh, and the pride of life. Instead, you acquired the understanding of Christ our Savior. We therefore appeal to your loving-kindness, that you will hear these praises which we now offer you.

Rejoice, for you were the peer of Saint Andrew, the Holy Fool for Christ.
Rejoice, for you renounced your own name, referring to yourself as dead.
Rejoice, for you assumed foolishness and took the name of your departed husband, Andrei.
Rejoice, for you called yourself by a man's name, renouncing pride and vanity.
Rejoice, for you accepted voluntary poverty for the sake of Christ.
Rejoice, for you distributed all your substance to good people and to the poor.
Rejoice, for you comfort all those who turn to you in prayer.
Rejoice, for you quickly help in times of trouble and despair.
Rejoice, for your holy foolishness has taught us to reject the vain wisdom of this age.
Rejoice, for you were full of wisdom transcending this world.

Rejoice, for you preferred mockery and ridicule to earthly glory.
Rejoice, for you have been glorified by God.
Rejoice, Blessed Xenia, faithful intercessor for our souls.

Kontakion 1

Blessed Mother Xenia, Holy Fool for the sake of Christ, you elected to undergo the struggle of patience and the suffering of affliction. We therefore honor your sacred memory with hymns of praise. Help us against our enemies, visible and invisible, that we may cry to you:

Rejoice, Blessed Xenia, faithful intercessor for our souls.

Prayer

Blessed Xenia, our patient and wise mother, you had no home or wealth in this world for you transcended all vanity and acquired the enlightenment of the Holy Spirit. You gave everything, materially and spiritually, to the poor. Since we are poor in every way, we call on you to direct us to the Lord Jesus Christ Who blessed your ascetic path with abundant wonders. You were regarded a homeless fool by the world, but you were a meek helper to the unfortunate and a builder of the Holy Church. Blessed mother, we implore your sympathy for our feeble resolve and our bitter troubles, for our daily tasks and our family relationships, and for our disabilities and our frailties. Have compassion upon us and spare us from sinister temptation and evil gloom. We request your kindness, and we thank you for your intercession. Amen.

Biography

The only record of "vital statistics" which has been left us concerning Blessed Xenia is the epitaph on her gravestone:

IN THE NAME OF THE FATHER, SON AND HOLY SPIRIT. HERE RESTS THE BODY OF THE SERVANT OF GOD, XENIA GRIGORIEVNA, WIFE OF THE IMPERIAL CHORISTER, COLONEL ANDREI THEODOROVICH PETROV. WIDOWED AT THE AGE OF 26, A PILGRIM FOR 45 YEARS, SHE LIVED A TOTAL OF 71 YEARS. SHE WAS KNOWN BY THE NAME ANDREI THEODOROVICH. MAY WHOEVER KNEW ME PRAY FOR MY SOUL THAT HIS OWN MAY BE SAVED. AMEN.

Little is known of her early life. Neither the dates of her birth nor of her death are known. Her birth is believed to have been about 1731 and her death about 1803.

The wife of Colonel Andrei Feodorovich Petrov, who served as a court chorister, Xenia fell into great grief upon the death of her husband when she was 26 years old. Appearing to have lost her mind from her grief, Xenia distributed her possessions to the poor, and keeping and dressing only in the clothes of her husband she wandered the streets of St Petersburg among the paupers. She called herself by her husband's name: Andrei Feodorovich. Her life was centered on God, seeking protection and comfort only in Him. During the nights, she refused refuge and went into the fields where she prayed through the nights.

When relatives of Xenia tried to help her with necessities she replied , "I do not need anything." The people of St. Petersburg came to love her as she placed the Kingdom of Heaven before earthly possessions. The people considered her presence in their homes as good signs. Her acceptance of services and bread from merchants, however small, brought them great sales as their customers, who loved the saintly Xenia, frequented those who helped her.

Xenia possessed the gift of clairvoyance. She foretold the deaths of the Empress Elizabeth, in 1761, and of the imprisoned John IV Antonovich, the great-great-grandson of Tsar Alexis, in 1764. After her death her grave became a place of pilgrimage. Portions of the dirt from her grave brought healing for many of the pilgrims.

Printed in Great Britain
by Amazon

38608162R00020